G-Thoughts

(Vol. 1)

G-Thoughts

(Vol. 1)

No Sunrise without Sunset

Satpal Singh Gill

PARTRIDGE
A Penguin Random House Company

To order additional copies of this book, contact
Partridge India
000 800 10062 62
www.partridgepublishing.com/india
orders.india@partridgepublishing.com

I dedicate this book to

My Dear Mother

"A mother is she who can take place of all others,
but whose place no one can take."

ACKNOWLEDGMENT

This book could not have completed without the help of some very important and special people. I would like to reiterate my thanks to everyone who took time to review this book and make invaluable suggestions. The list is endless. Let me name a few.

- God
- My Teachers
- My Family members
- My Relatives
- My Friends
- My Well-wishers
- My Students
- My Staff members
- Microsoft
- Publisher of this book

Last and not least, I beg forgiveness of all those who have been with me during this project, but I forget to mention their names.

PREFACE

The need of self motivation cannot be denied in this fast running world. It's not sufficient to be successful, but more importantly it is the hunger of an individual to be happily successful. "No Sunrise without Sunset" is a book of 500 inspiring thoughts, which has the power to change your life-style positively and help to make your dreams become realities. From these 500 thoughts, you will find many which depicts your life. Please do not just read the thought and forget, but from 500 thoughts, even if you apply one to your life, you had helped the author in completing the very purpose of the book.

"To err is human." The author apologizes for all the things those went wrong (if any) in making the things right. Feel free to use or share the thoughts given in the book.

1. No sunrise without sunset.

2. Going against our heart, no matter how logical a course of action might appear does not yield happiness.

3. Through every disrespectful fight that happens between a husband and a wife, they issue a license to their children to disrespect them.

4. By allowing ourselves to be different, we give ourselves permission to be excellent, instead of being ordinary.

5. If you do not get what you want when you want it, and it disturbs you, it has gained mastery over you.

6. Do not accept anyone's definition of life, define it yourself. After all, it is your life, and this is the only chance you have got, to be you.

7. You cannot get your life right by speaking about what is wrong all the time.

8.   The moment you reach the destination station, no fun is there to drink a cup of coffee. Enjoy the coffee, while in travel.

9.   Love yourself, for you will never be able to love anyone else otherwise.

10. God is like a potter, who continuously hits the pot from the outside to give it shape, yet has supporting hand inside all the while.

11. On your birthday, you were gifted to this world and this world was gifted to you. Don't miss the world and let this world not miss you.

12. The aim of your 'must' be to become the 'being' you can be.

13. After failing twice, Edmund Hilary said to Everest, "I'll come again and conquer you, because as a mountain, you can't grow, but as a human, I can." That's Attitude.

14.   We order an item from the menu card and seeing what the person on the adjacent table is eating we think, 'may be I should have ordered that.'

15.   Some people pray in life. For some, life itself is prayer.

16.   Play to win and not to defeat.

17.   List of problems often do not require a list of solutions. Few solutions will solve many problems.

18.   A friend can dare to say you even those secrets, he hesitate to whisper onto himself.

19.   You lose a lot more by not taking the risk than by taking the risk.

20.   Success is never 'somehow', but is always 'how'.

21.   Ironically, by being themselves, the history makers lifted the rest of the

world more than all the history readers put together.

22. It doesn't matter how poor a man is; if he has a family, he's rich.

23. Working sincerely for your office, even when there is nobody to notice it or appreciate it, is nothing less than a prayer.

24. The happiness we experience in making others happy is far greater than the happiness we get through any other means.

25. There is no secured freedom. Either settle for secured slavery or choose insecure freedom.

26. There is no point in keeping the 'exit' door open all the time.

27. Time management is first an attitude and only then a skill.

28. Out of six and a half billion actors on the stage of this world, not one can play your role better than you.

29. A home is the place where welcoming arms will pick the kids up when they fall flat on their face.

30. The most dangerous and scariest creature on this earth that has destroyed millions of relationships and caused havoc in uncountable lives is ENVY.

31. There has never been another you. There will never be another you. You are the only one of your kind. You are rare, unique and original. Celebrate your originality. Let the world remark, "I met a man who did not remind me of anybody else."

32. Every distraction enhances your ability to stay attracted to what you choose to focus upon.

33. It is not a question of not having expectations, but having the right kind and realistic kind of expectations.

34. God wants to help us, but very often we make ourselves not worthy of His help.

35. Depending on the role that we play, the definition of our home takes a different dimension and direction.

36. The ways of a teacher, a teacher alone understands.

37. All of us can bask in the sun and nothing of the sun is ever lost. We can love all and yet the love that fountains from an embodiment of love never diminishes.

38. Remember, your mother thinks you're cute, even if no one else.

39. It is not God, who is making your faith work. It is your faith, that is making your God work.

40. Spirituality must be your strength, and not become your weakness.

41. Recognizing the heart behind the material makes it a gift. Even a gift is just a material, if you don't see the heart behind the material.

42. When you avoid what you must face, the situation becomes bigger than you and takes control over you. When you face what you must face, you become bigger than the situation and you take control over it.

43. Why would you sell your hair to buy a comb?

44. You listen best when you have nothing more to say.

45. Difficulties and disappointments are the events which lead us to maturity.

46. Wake up before sunrise—people who wake up late miss one of the greatest gifts of nature.

47. Problems in relationships occur because each person is concentrating on what is missing in the other person.

48. An unburdened mind is a receptive mind.

49. When a seed stays rooted in the soil long enough, it will develop roots and eventually grow into a tree. However, if I keep unearthing the seed every few days and keep re-planting it in different places, it will not even become a plant.

50. After quality time, the second best gift you can give to your kids is the gift of a good example.

51. Only when you feel responsible for your life, you can respond with ability. Else, it will be responding with disability.

52. Every seed is a potential forest, but so many factors beyond the seed determine, whether it will grow to its entire potential.

53.   Everything comes to us that belong to us, if we create the capacity to receive it.

54.   Everyone desires success but everyone does not succeed, and the difference is rather simple and obvious—does he have the 'how' on paper before putting his best foot forward?

55.   Even the best of performers today, needed a stage sometime back.

56.   Irrespective of our motivation, moods and choices, the clock ticks at the same speed.

57.   The feel that 'I know the subject' will stop you from gaining deeper insights on the subject.

58.   We always dream of a better quality of life, yet do nothing to make it better!

59.   You cannot live your today with the perceptions that were formed yesterday.

60. There is a need to pray during bad times, but it is a must to pray during good times with more sincerity and intensity so that the good times last forever.

61. The question is not 'out of everything which is the best' but, 'how to get the best out of everything?'

62. The cycle of change is such that before change you are comfortable; after change you will again be comfortable; but the transition is never comfortable.

63. A helicopter can take you to the top of Mount Everest, but nothing can ever replace the experience of having climbed it.

64. What is cultivated is called a crop. What grows by itself is a weed.

65. Man not only has the power to take responsibility for his own life, but has within him the capacity to take responsibility for the life of others too.

66. When you identify yourself with a cause larger than yourself, the energy and competence that are required for the fulfillment of the cause comes seeking you.

67. 'Getting what you want' is one form of blessing. 'Not getting what you didn't want' is another form of a blessing.

68. Educate your daughters and encourage them to dream, aspire and achieve, because when you educate a girl, you educate a family, a community and finally the nation.

69. We are not human beings leading spiritual lives, but spiritual beings leading human lives and the spirit never dies.

70. It is not badge of honor to be a 'fault' finder. It takes an 'able' minded and 'noble' hearted person to be a 'good' finder.

71. Growth is not always adding something to our self. A good amount of growth comes from letting go of false views.

72. This life is given to us not to possess and own, but to love and give and share whatever we have with those less fortunate than us.

73. From under a heap of garbage, a banyan seed that refused to remain hidden emerged into a huge banyan tree to awaken the land around it.

74. You get married not to be happy, but to make each other happy.

75. You can't keep behaving small and expect to become big in life.

76. The moment you say, 'A worthy book', words like 'affordable' and 'spending' automatically go out of the window.

77. This is a beautiful world and with our human qualities we can make it a wonderful one.

78. Peace is not something that needs to be achieved at the end. It is a state that needs to be experienced even when I am in progress.

79. It is far better to get a personality and develop a professional, instead of recruiting a professional and struggling to create a personality.

80. All troubles eventually end. So why be troubled by troubles?

81. You have only one life to live. Even if you are reborn, you will not be born as you. Don't miss yourself.

82. Every child is a reflection of the parenting that's gone in.

83. A good teacher not only teaches a subject, but also teaches the students how to live life.

84. Incompetence is not when I cannot do what others do. Incompetence is when I do not do what I am capable of doing.

85. Dreams backed up by sincere efforts are sure to give you success.

86. Beware! Expertise is the enemy of learning.

87. The heart desires the goal and now the mind has to lay out the process of 'how'.

88. The higher and higher you go in life, you understand that it is 'nothing of you and everything of Him'.

89. Don't fear because someone tried and fail, but fear that if you fail, someone won't try.

90. The way you look at everything around you when you are secure is so different from how you look at everything otherwise.

91. Open communication helps you to either clarify or get clarified.

92.   When right quantum of time goes to the right activities, then you will get your life right.

93.   When you don't give up, you go up.

94.   It is not in being born as a human being, but it is in living as a human being, we live a human life.

95.   Man is the only creation capable of leaving a legacy and to live beyond his lifetime.

96.   Not knowing God is not ignorance. Actually, trying to understand God is ignorance.

97.   When we consciously focus on the things that make us happy and devote time to it, our problems will start looking small.

98.   Money in the hands of a bad human being will destroy the existing world. Money in the hands of a good human being will create a new world.

99. If you have faith, why worry? If you worry, why have faith?

100. Forgiveness means telling yourself, "I value my peace more than anything that has happened to me in my life."

101. Life is like a book where you write your story, but just remember you don't have an eraser.

102. A seed, born as a seed, will live all its life as a seed and die as a seed, if it does not find soil to grow.

103. By feeling His presence constantly, we can experience the quality of life changing.

104. In every person's career, there are times when earning takes precedence over learning and times when learning takes priority over earning.

105. Man is not a creature of logic, but a creature of emotions.

106. Never make your today the enemy of your tomorrow.

107. Dissatisfaction is the gap between actual and expectations.

108. The intention with which you write and the way you form a sentence can have altogether a different meaning in the mind of the person who reads it.

109. To move at a snail's pace is success to the snail, but not to the rabbit.

110. When you resist what is happening in life, what is happening in life continues to happen, creating misery in you. When you accept what is happening in life, what is happening in life continues to happen, leaving you blissful.

111. Life is all about the journey from 'incompleteness' to 'completeness'.

112. 'What you become' means nothing if it comes at the cost of 'who you are'.

113. The more you enjoy your health, sooner than later you will find your body expressing the same through good health.

114. The answer of a responsible teacher is much more relevant to the questioner than the question.

115. Proper physical exercise increases your chances for health, and proper mental exercise increases your chances for wealth.

116. Old age can become a pleasure if one chooses to keep himself engaged in areas that interest him.

117. Life does not give a tenth standard exam paper to a ninth standard student. Life gives the right test to the right student, because it will help the student to grow and reach the next standard.

118. To sustain the depth of a relationship, especially marriage, from the very

beginning relate to the person and not just the body.

119. Instead of accepting yourself as you are and expecting the world to change, accept the world as it is and you start changing your approach towards the world.

120. Good always comes back to those who send it others' way.

121. It is far better to live a life of trial and error than to lead a life of regrets.

122. Life's challenges aren't there to stifle you. In fact, they serve you and help you to discover who you are.

123. Unproductive anger that depletes our energy is something to be avoided through maturity.

124. Everything will appear scratched, if there is a scratch in the spectacles through which you view life.

125. In a successful marriage, whenever she goes to 'her' space and comes to 'our' space, that's when she is at her best in 'our' space. The same is true with him.

126. God is not a matter of belief; God is a matter of alignment.

127. The very fact that so many failures have finally turned into success implies that failures are not wrong.

128. Your own value is determined not by what you are, but by what you are able to make of yourself.

129. Greatness of character does not lie in thinking positive when everything is going like a song, but in thinking positive when things are going deadly wrong.

130. If we waste time thinking about the dirt around, when will we have time to clean up the mess and maintain what is good?

131. Trouble in marriage often starts when a man gets so busy earning his salt that he forgets his sugar.

132. To live life with a complete sense of freedom, 'Go to any relationship, looking at WHAT YOU CAN GIVE and not WHAT YOU CAN RECEIVE.'

133. Your tomb will read what you have done, and not what you could have.

134. An optometrist can correct your eyesight with the right pair of glasses, but only a guru can give you vision.

135. Don't look at what has left you; look at what you are left with.

136. The more I run away from a problem, the more difficult it is to resolve.

137. it's better to start over again than to give up entirely.

138. You are not the only one going through what you go through.

139. The more and more we process the thoughts, 'my health is my responsibility', we become accountable to it.

140. Oxygen is always there, but you need to inhale. Gravity is in action always, but you need to be aligned. God is always . . . but, are you a devotee always?

141. 'Once' is life's responsibility. To make it 'Always' is man's responsibility.

142. No one can take responsibility for your life, like you can.

143. Your life does not change when others change. Your life changes when you change.

144. Get the man in you right, the world will automatically become right.

145. When we are young we talk about what we will do, when we are older and when

we are old, we talk about what we did, when we were young.

146. Fear is expanded 'False Evidence Accepted Real', face it with faith, which is 'Face Anything In Trusting Him'.

147. Let's realize the value of what we have when we still have it, instead of repenting when it's gone.

148. Expecting your partner to be perfect is imperfection on your side.

149. When your energies are focused on your improvement, rather than trying to improve the world around you, it becomes a journey of self-discovery, an adventure in self-empowerment.

150. The core character trait of every revolutionary is disobedience.

151. When your little ones throw tantrums, they are not giving you a hard time; instead they are having a hard time.

152. When we are able to understand the context in which the other is trying to communicate, we would be able to understand the spirit of the communication.

153. Happiness is a decision we should take much before encountering a situation.

154. The world belongs to those with 'Horizontal exposure and Vertical expertise'—exposed to many things with specialization in one.

155. The fear of denial is a natural fear that seems to overshadow most people and this instinctive emotion paralyses us from attracting huge possibilities.

156. There are certain moments in life, that are too special and such moments happen only a few times in an entire lifetime.

157. What is 'good' need not always be 'important' and what is 'important' need not always be 'good'. However, it is

important to know that investing time in 'good' is always 'important'.

158. Our contributions and our creations should continue to live in this world and the world should continue to benefit from the life we lived, even much after we are physically gone.

159. Just as we cannot plant new crops without first pulling out the old roots, we need to unlearn before we can learn a new.

160. To see yourself, do not look to the mirror; look into the eyes of the people.

161. Teaching actually keeps the student within alive.

162. Make the right investments in your 'Today', and script wonderful 'Tomorrow'.

163. If you don't believe in yourself, then there is no force in this universe that can lead you through.

164. Grow in such a way, that one day all those people who rejected you will admire you.

165. It is not a question of being firm or being kind to the children; the need in parenting is to be 'kind and firm'.

166. Start appreciating what you have and stop counting what you don't have.

167. Look around and find out! You can always be instrumental in making someone realize his or her forgotten dream.

168. After every mistake, correct the system that allowed the mistake.

169. Let your fear of failure not prevent you from you daring to step into the unknown future of infinite possibilities.

170. Accepting yourself as you are is the very first step towards transformation.

171. If your today is no different from your yesterday, then your tomorrow is not going to be any better than your today.

172. Without process excellence, there can never be excellence in results.

173. We human beings have the basic nature of celebrating the disease by attaching too much emotion and too much attention to it and hence life keeps giving more of what we celebrate.

174. Criticism or feedback should always be accepted with a 'thank you' and not 'sorry'.

175. Making and honoring commitments is a very powerful tool in actualizing and maximizing one's potential.

176. Disobedience doesn't always mean disrespect.

177. There are no magic pills to achieve good health. Good health calls for time, attention and lifestyle modifications.

178. A person who can speak many languages is not necessarily more valuable than a person who can listen in one.

179. No matter what challenges God gives you, He will be there to help you through it.

180. If you want to achieve anything big in life, then your body needs to cooperate with you and for that to happen, you need to be careful of what you eat.

181. We have one of two choices: Either change by inspiring ourselves to see the light, or life will force us to feel the heat and change.

182. A simple gesture from a heart overflowing with love and happiness can communicate more than all the words that come from the lips.

183. Pray, "Oh Lord, this day of mine is your gift unto me and the way I live this day will be my gift unto you."

184. Right amount of workout, right food and adequate rest will give one good health. When the basics go wrong, everything goes wrong.

185. The most essential quality of a good coach is not that he has to be better than you, but he should be a great observer and a reader of you.

186. Be grateful to God for He allowed you to suffer in order to learn a lesson in life that you needed to learn, and then thank Him again for restarting your faith so as to enable you to see the new beginning of your life.

187. We might not have born healthy, but we can certainly live a healthy life.

188. We can train our mind to immediately think positive whenever we face a stressful situation.

189. Just because we feel something, doesn't mean God is present, and just

because we don't feel anything, doesn't mean God is absent.

190.   Faith grows with time. Beliefs weaken in time.

191.   It is better to explain the price once, than to apologize for the lack of quality every time.

192.   If we focus on our 'abundance', scarcity will leave this earth eventually.

193.   The more and more reasons I find to laugh, the fewer and fewer are the reasons I find to get pulled down.

194.   If I keep comparing myself with others at every point of time, at one point I will become them. It makes sense, if that is the ultimate aim, else it is worthless.

195.   We enjoy what we accumulate in a lifetime, but the world enjoys what we create and leave behind.

196. Gratefulness alone helps start your life beyond scarcity, instead of from scarcity.

197. You don't need new horizons. You just need the right spectacles with which you can see the existing horizons.

198. Our daunted faith that He will not give us a challenge which we cannot handle will help us pass through the rough storm.

199. Never look for that perfect someone to love. Instead look for that imperfect someone and love him perfectly.

200. Instead of curing the headache, it's better to cure the thing that caused it.

201. Every product has an end-user, but the art of finding the end-user is a challenge.

202. A man was holding a bull by the rope and he was convinced that he had enslaved the bull. True, the bull never

run away from him; but little did he realize that neither he can run away from the bull. Your slave enslaves you.

203. Life is a beautiful gift, provided we don't ration out its abilities.

204. When you get the man within you right, the world you see outside of you will look right.

205. Only the person of worth can recognize the worth in others.

206. When you are doing something and people tell you that it's not practical, tell them that you are putting it into practice, so that next time when somebody else do the same, it's practical.

207. Boredom and monotony is because you think life is repetitive, but life in its very design cannot repeat itself.

208. By causing fear in the child you may succeed to get him to study, but that

little one will fight a lifetime to overcome his fear.

209. Success is just an empty success if you don't create moments of celebration around it.

210. Today, take a moment and think about the people in your life who need to be cherished, appreciated and told that their support has been helpful.

211. A new form of religion in itself means that the founder of the new religion chose to disobey the old religious practices that were practiced until then.

212. The word religion has its Latin roots— RE LIGARE, that is RE (again) and LIGARE (to reconnect).

213. There are no shortcuts in the laws of nature.

214. Your coach may not be able to achieve what you may be able to achieve, but

his achievement lies in making you an achiever.

215. "When I see it, I will believe it", is an old paradigm. "Only when you believe in it, you will see it", is the truth.

216. Best friends don't ask you, "Is something wrong?" Best friends ask you, "What's wrong?"

217. There is greater freedom of not being judgmental and it improves our ability to appreciate and respect others.

218. When the need to 'have' expresses itself, man desires to possess and the selfishness within him gains expression. When the need to 'give' expresses itself, man desires to share and the unselfishness within him finds expression.

219. The problem with ego is that when ego is fed, you struggle with a superiority complex, and when ego is starved you

suffer from an inferiority complex. Either way, it robs you of your peace of mind.

220. Most of the time, man sees life as a problem, because he does not take stock of the available resources with which he can overcome the situation.

221. When we stop celebrating the success, life doesn't give us enough success to celebrate further.

222. A coacher may not be able to achieve what you may achieve, but a coach's achievement is in making you an achiever. After all, to train a dog, I should know how to train a dog. I don't have to be a dog.

223. So many times, success is just one step ahead when people give up.

224. Remember, we have an unwritten social contract with the rest of humanity.

225. People who fight for causes are never concerned about happiness or unhappiness.

226. Food is meant to enhance your life, not diminish it. So take it wisely.

227. Difficulties are uninvited guests that should be received warmly.

228. If asked, you won't crush 24 rupees and throw it in the dustbin. Yet, so many 24 hours are dumped aimlessly.

229. The stronger the head becomes, the softer the heart needs to be.

230. You live only once as you, and if you miss this chance, you will never have another opportunity to be yourself.

231. When we keep having positive thoughts from our childhood, the chances of having a control on our life will be higher.

232. Nothing comes easy in life and anything good in life comes with a price and once we have decided to make it big, we will have to burn the midnight oil, dirty our hands and sometimes sacrifice our personal interests.

233. Memories of the 'firsts' are always special, and they enjoy a very special place in our hearts.

234. What are relationships for, if you can't even tell a person, he is wrong when you feel he is wrong?

235. Even between the words health and wealth, 'h' comes first in alphabet.

236. Let us shift from the attitude of 'I must do it' to 'I want to do it'.

237. Existence always challenges her favorite creation—man, so that he can discover the stuff he is made of.

238. The only way to show our love for the Messenger is by living His message.

239. The world comes in search of happy people.

240. Don't depend too much on the elevator that you forget to use the stairs.

241. Certainty provides order. Uncertainty provides growth. Both order and growth are needed to complete life.

242. More than your own success, the success of those you create is always dearer to you.

243. Unless man experiences evil he is ignorant of good.

244. Ego is 'everything of me and nothing of you'. Surrender is 'nothing of me and everything of you'.

245. What is the point in overburdening ourselves with tomorrow's challenges today? After all, what can be done tomorrow can be done only tomorrow!

246. The whole of human history is like an unlimited drama, and each one of us have our unique role to play.

247. Bitterness about the past is not merely negative—it is destructive and self-destructive.

248. Doing anything in a relaxed state puts our body and mind in peak state. Doing anything in a tensed and restless state not only accelerates the aging of the body, but also puts the mind into a confused state.

249. When you give in to your fears and failures you fall in your own eyes; when you stand up in spite of your fears and failures, you grow in your own eyes.

250. Growing up is automatic, but maturating is a matter of choice.

251. It's foolish to keep expecting all the time from life, for it takes away the lingering of the surprise.

252. If an idea is worth it, then all the resources that are needed for the fulfillment of that idea, on their own accord, come together.

253. It doesn't matter how many times you go through a holy book. But what is important is that the holy book should go through you at least once.

254. Wherever opportunities present themselves, be the first one to put your hand up.

255. Don't say 'yes' or 'no' to anything; 'yes' attaches you, 'no' repulses you. They don't lead you to the truth. Take from both whatever promotes your search for truth.

256. Go to bed praying and get up singing and notice what a fine day's work you will do.

257. The actions of parents can be debated, but never their intentions. They are truly our character architects.

258. Every pawn is just six moves away from becoming the queen—the most powerful piece on the board.

259. When you 'have' a personality, you do not 'have to wear' a personality.

260. The judgment of others on what you are capable of doing and not capable of doing is born more out of their background and not yours.

261. If we don't identify our purpose in life, we will only add days to our lives and not life to our days.

262. 'Anywhere' or 'only here' both take the same time to keep a thing, but at the time of retrieval, 'only here' is economy of effort.

263. It is never a question of whether you are right or I am right; it is a question of what is right and fair for everyone concerned.

264. No matter how the world has been for us till yesterday, let's begin every today with the belief, "This world is becoming a much better, safer and beautiful place to live in".

265. Create so many happy memories that all the challenges of life look like small and insignificant events in front of them.

266. It needs courage to run completely in a different direction.

267. When you pose a question, "Who am I?" to yourself, initially the mind would deceive you with fake answers. But, hold the question long enough. It will do miracles.

268. The hammer that shatters glass forges steel. So, what troubles and challenges do to you depends on who you are and how you see them.

269. A home is the place where we allow our children to lead their lives the way they want to.

270. Blessed are those, who have understood, that they should be loving people and using things, and not loving things and using people.

271. It's nice to do good in front of others, but what you do when no one's around, defines who you really are.

272. Everything that comes into our life should either stay with us to become our strength, or it should leave us to make us free. It should never stay with us and become our weakness.

273. If you are comfortable with sharing silence with someone, you can comfortably share just about everything else with him/her.

274. It is only when we discover our weaknesses that we are indeed strong.

275. Leadership is in challenging people to go beyond their perceived limitations, and thus reveal unto them that they are better than they think they are.

276.   We don't have to be too bothered about the weeds, if we can ensure that we have abundant sprouting from the seeds.

277.   To fall is not a mistake; to not try and rise after the fall is a mistake.

278.   However secure it may be, there is no meaning in staying in the womb.

279.   People, who do not trust you before the explanation, will not trust you even after the explanation.

280.   Several inventions and discoveries that we enjoy today wouldn't have been possible, had the people behind it set a target of giving up.

281.   Qualification can give you a head start in your career, but the leader who leads by the philosophy that there are no 'no solution' situations is the leader of the future.

282. Only when we believe in ourselves, the existential force will lead us through.

283. There may not be happiness in wealth, but there is considerable wealth in the experience of happiness.

284. However ornate the coffin is, when it holds merely a dead body, it is not attractive. On the other hand, if that decoration is given to the cradle holding a bubbly child, the impact of life will be far reaching.

285. Becoming spiritual does not mean sitting in a church or temple 24 hours a day. It means living in the awareness that, I the soul, is a spiritual being, the child of God and all souls are my brothers and sisters.

286. Irrespective of the consequences, have the courage to be honest.

287. It is always better to have good manners than good looks.

288. Good communication will serve a relationship; improper communication will sever a relationship.

289. The body takes time to adjust, the mind takes longer, but the heart takes the longest to adapt.

290. So much of the spirit of our lives is written by us, depending on how we respond in the 'Now'.

291. When love depends on 'what you do' and 'what you don't', it disturbs the flow in relationship.

292. It is important to shift focus from what is causing trouble to how to survive this threat.

293. God is not a person, who has to be pleased all the time, but a system to which you need to align yourself.

294. You can never make a person happy who is not at peace with himself. And, you can never be at peace with

yourself, if you want everyone to be happy with you.

295. Where I invest my time today will define where my progress will be tomorrow.

296. Don't give too much attention to diseases. It takes more space in your subconscious and it will keep on conspiring against you and keeps giving you experiences of diseases.

297. A home is a place where all the members get their own space.

298. It is necessary that everyone completes the task assigned to him to perfection with full involvement to maintain balance on earth.

299. Problems are thrown at us so that we can grow, so that we can evolve.

300. Do you know which the best part of your life is? When your family understands you as a friend and your friends support you as your family.

301. It is only when I am in peace, it will be considered as progress and not otherwise.

302. If you get stressed because of your responsibilities, you cannot respond with ability.

303. What you are capable of is defined by the infinite potential sleeping within you.

304. Self-belief is not built by giving speeches to a child. It is built by giving the child victorious experiences.

305. The challenge at one point will seem like a blessing at a later point in time.

306. Anything done out of unhappiness will only bring multiplied unhappiness.

307. Good marriages do not just happen. They are created by dedicated effort— effort, not to find WHO is wrong, but to find out WHAT is wrong.

308. There comes a time in every person's life, when he or she must learn to say no to good ideas, because something that is good and something that is right are not always the same thing.

309. If you yourself don't know how to live, then how are you going to let others live?

310. Do something to be proud of today, because tomorrow may not come.

311. Friends, Health and Time—these things don't come with price tag, but when we lose them, we realize the cost.

312. Begin everyday with the question, "What is that I can do better today?" End everyday with the question, "Where have I improved today?"

313. Treat a man as he is, and you will keep him here. Instead, treat him as he can be, and you will help him to reach there.

314. What cannot be achieved with happiness, can never be achieved out of unhappiness.

315. It's hard to believe that we live in a world, where most people are more concerned with following the crowd and doing what everyone else is doing than living their own dreams.

316. Unless food is cooked happily, served happily and eaten happily, it does not become health.

317. For want of resources, do not miss out on opportunities. Resources can be managed, but opportunities must not be missed.

318. It all depends on the quality you bring to your actions rather than the action itself.

319. How can you give the world something that you haven't first gifted to yourself?

320. Unknown is the parenthesis inside which infinite opportunities hide themselves.

321. The effect is nothing but the cause itself in a different form.

322. The beauty of a master communicator lies not just in his ability to pack his oration with words, but also in punctuating his delivery with appropriate pauses.

323. As long as we know we have genuine well wishers and sources of inspiration, no battle is too big to be won.

324. The inability of the world to accept abundant trait in any form is the limitation of the world, and not yours.

325. What foolishness it is to accumulate something with which peace can never be purchased or preserved!

326. Relationships can triumph or conditions can triumph; both cannot.

327. True growth is only when your own past seems like someone else's past.

328. Every time you experience success thank God and proceed; every time you experience failure take lessons and proceed.

329. A bad man may get his way through, but in seeing everyone as a potential bad, you will miss a million good people.

330. What is that one thing that you want to do for the rest of your life irrespective of whether you are recognized or not?

331. When you are with books, you are actually having a date with the great souls.

332. Everything that has happened to you in your life—the good and the difficult was necessary to help you become the person, you are now.

333. Good becomes best in the hands of right leadership.

334. Find a work that gives you the inner expression, you will find happiness in it. Make the world recognize the value you add through your work, you will find success in it. Use your success to serve the world, you will find purpose in it. And, when your work gives you happiness, success and purpose, you will find God in it.

335. Deadlines exist everywhere, but it is important whether we are associating pain or pleasure with the deadline.

336. Have this faith that no parent will ever give his child a story to read, if it doesn't have a happy ending and play the game of life courageously.

337. Never can there be a moment of marriage between ego and ease.

338. Discover one thing worth fighting for, and then never ever give up.

339. The beauty about 'Today' is, as much as it is the effect of the past, it is also the cause for the 'Tomorrow'.

340. On this planet earth, there is nobody who does only mistakes or there is nobody who never does a mistake.

341. While following our heart cannot guarantee success, not following our heart cannot guarantee lasting fulfillment.

342. What is good for me need not necessarily be good for someone and what is bad for me need not necessarily be bad for the other.

343. A guru is that sublime relationship of your life that connects you to the divine.

344. For understanding to happen, words must have the same meaning to the listener as well as the communicator.

345. A parent who does one thing, but expects or demands the opposite

from his child is more likely to face challenges in disciplining the child.

346. The mother bird knows instinctively when exactly it should push the baby bird out of the nest, so that it will learn to fly.

347. An angry man is crying for a perfect world, a world he is never going to find.

348. Exercise helps you to look at life in a fresh way.

349. Those who seek an answer to the question, 'Where is God' are too busy to forget that God cannot be contained in something, but is present in everything and nothing.

350. With strength when you think, solutions shall come; with weakness if you think, only tears will come.

351. We are completely ignorant of the fact that we must 'live our life' and to

live our life, we ought to make viable decisions at the right time.

352. Protect your elders and they will give their lives for your well-being. Their recipe is always simple to make, tasty to eat and easy to digest.

353. Laying your hands on the right book is as good as finding a great friend in your life.

354. The high tide cannot always remain there—it has to come down.

355. Change, by itself is a relaxing experience, and a relaxed mind always thinks well.

356. If life is so important, life-related policies—the values of life are even more important.

357. The fact of life is that everything evens out over a period of time.

358. Deep relationships are not built by making others understand you, but in giving others the confidence that you have understood them.

359. Defeat may lead to the development of a stronger willpower, provided one accepts it as a challenge to greater effort and not as a signal to stop trying.

360. You learn the biggest lessons in life through small and the simplest things.

361. When a painter starts thinking 'Will the world accept this concept', even before trying to paint, he'll never be able to create a masterpiece.

362. Let this question always linger in your being, "When was the last time, I did something for the first time?'

363. We must not let our personal disturbances, big or small, affect the people who are dependent on us.

364. If all the work I do becomes my offering unto my God, then my very life becomes a prayer unto Him.

365. History suggests that one man is enough to be a turning point in this world.

366. You say, "I like eating." Precisely for the same reason, eat less; you will live long enough to eat.

367. When people are emotional about their problems, it isn't the time to talk solutions; it is time for protective love.

368. We seem to always miss all the living masters and prophets when they are around and then spend lifetimes catching up after they are gone.

369. The speed of the train is the speed of the engine. If the man at the top is not growing, he slows down the whole organization.

370. Love is love, only when, what you do and what you do not do does not alter my love for you. We call that unconditional love. If love is not unconditional, then it is not love at all.

371. We need to dedicate time and space in our daily routines to do something that gives us joy, peace and happiness.

372. Only if your intentions are noble, then existence takes over to do the rest.

373. Knowingly or unknowingly, if you are aligned, God works with you, by whatever name you choose to call him.

374. Where is the pain of running the marathon, when you are experiencing the pleasure of having gone past the finishing line?

375. Every day, before you think of your long list of prayer requests, thank God for all what he's already done!

376. If courage means going ahead 'in spite of', then courage also means staying back 'because of.'

377. Faith is 'it will be done', not 'when it will be done.'

378. By law of existence, you cannot desire for yourself, what you despise for others and you cannot despise for yourself, what you desire for others.

379. In spite of the canvass, despite the paints and the brushes involved, the quality of a painting is the responsibility of a painter.

380. Best lines said by a mathematician: "My love for my friend is like a circle. It has no sides to be broken, no ends to be ended, and no angles to be measured."

381. Compared to the infinite human potential each one of us is bestowed with, can any situation about life be termed a problem?

382. When you play the game with a player who is less skilled than you, even if you keep winning, your game does not improve. However, when you play the game with a player who is better than you, even if you keep losing, your game keeps improving.

383. The most powerful instrument that mankind possess is thought power, which is more powerful than the nuclear weapons.

384. We should prefer to invest time to appreciate the beauty and fragrance of the rose instead of worrying about the thorns.

385. Even if you have to slow down, slow down; but keep moving.

386. The game of life is tough, but it isn't a game that cannot be won.

387. Children respect their parents not based on who is successful, but purely based

on whether their parents respect each other.

388. What you leave behind your children is not important; what you leave in your children is important.

389. Life need not change, but your outlook towards life needs to change.

390. History is full of simple human beings who won over forces well beyond their control and emerged as champions.

391. Your workplace can find a replacement for you, but your family cannot.

392. Whether the world encourages or discourages you makes no difference; whether you encourage or discourage yourself makes all the difference.

393. Only if we are mature enough, unselfish enough and receptive enough to understand that, it is not a question of my way or your way, it is a question of adopting a way which will benefit all the

people concerned, will the relationship blossom.

394. Achieving the desired purpose through communication is possible only when you touch the heart of the other.

395. So often, people who need the solution the most, heed to it the least.

396. 'Somebody misappropriated funds' is only half the story. 'Some loopholes where there in the system that allowed misappropriation' is the other half of the story.

397. When you begin to stand for yourself, the world begins to stand up for you.

398. Do not worry or be anxious about tomorrow for tomorrow will have worries and anxieties of its own.

399. Being proud of your country is not enough. Resolve to do something in your lifetime, that your country will be proud of . . .

400. When the head of an organization is not loyal to his chair, it jeopardizes the whole organization.

401. Living life by continuously renewing your perceptions is to design one's own heart.

402. Try to use every opportunity you have now, because you can't turn back the hand of time.

403. One needs to treat his body as a friend and listen to what it needs.

404. Life ends everything that has begun and begins everything to eventually end it.

405. When you hold your peace above everything else, nothing and no one can disturb you. When you hold your ego above everything else, then everything and everyone disturbs you.

406. Nobody will ask, where the son would be without their mother, but everybody

would ask, where the mother would be without their son.

407. If you are happy, it does not mean others are unhappy. If you are sad, it does not mean others are sad.

408. Life calls upon you and gives you experiences repeatedly to prove who you are by demonstrating who you are not.

409. As long as we can remain His instrument, our life will be rhythmically flowing music.

410. What you are as a person, whether it be success or failure, depends to a large degree upon your personal habits.

411. Faith is the ability to trust what you are not able to see, the ability to believe what is not yet, the ability to accept as true that which cannot be proven.

412. Confidence is not about knowing how much of your surrounding you are

aware of, but in knowing how much of you that you are aware of.

413. One of the best childhood memory—it was magic. It doesn't matter if you sleep on a sofa, or floor, or anywhere, you will always wake up on bed.

414. On the road, the responsibility of 'not hitting' and 'not being hit', both are yours and yours alone.

415. When we believe that life should not give us difficult tests and challenges because we have been good people and haven't harmed anyone, then those very tests will appear severe, unfair and unjust and will become more difficult to handle. When we believe that life's tests are not punishments, but life's way of grooming us because it wants to take us to the next level, then those very tests will be less difficult to handle.

416. Hurt destroys both, the one who caused it and the one who is hurt.

417. We will definitely wake up to the loss of a loved one someday and at that point it would be too late to repent.

418. The seed has to sprout and fight against the forces of the earth to emerge above the soil.

419. The beauty of human nature is this affirming belief—'it won't happen to me'.

420. The truth is even God cannot change the way we choose to emotionally react to a situation. When we realize this, we become more responsible for our emotions and stop blaming the world for our moods.

421. Time brings all of us to a stage in life when your own past seems like someone else's life.

422. The Guru allows you to love him not because he needs your love, but because something within you gets purified in loving him.

423. Have we become so much of a public property, that we cannot have some private moments with ourselves?

424. A home is the place where our kids know, that they will get total support for their beliefs.

425. Out of hundred aspects of life, if ninety are going great, then that is enough reason to be happy.

426. To know that we know what we know and we do not know what we do not know is the true knowledge.

427. A house becomes a home because there is a vital ingredient called love in it.

428. Your old strengths in a new environment become your new weaknesses.

429. To be interested in the body of those to whom you cannot rightfully gift motherhood or fatherhood, is not right. To feel with the body of the one to

whom you will cause motherhood or fatherhood is rightfully right.

430. The inability to move at a rabbit's pace isn't a snail's failure.

431. Competition helps you to raise the bar of your own standards.

432. Much after we are physically gone, we can continue to live spiritually through the legacy we create and leave behind.

433. Every decision goes either the 'right' way or the 'wrong' way. It is much easier to go the wrong way, but it gets tougher as we go along. It may be tough to go the right way, but it gets easier as we go along.

434. Every man in a small way is the image of God.

435. Just as every person has a unique personality, everyone is entitled to create his own definition of happiness.

436. If I am thinking of someone's weaknesses and defeats, I may become uneasy and depressed and irritated. If I am thinking of someone's good qualities, I begin to feel lightness and easiness within my mind.

437. It is only when all inner chatter stops, creativity and spontaneity untouched by past noise will emerge from the depth of the unknown.

438. Where conditions take the front row, relationships take a back seat. Where relations take the front row, conditions take a back seat.

439. The only way to erase a negative is to produce enough counter positives.

440. According to holy books, it takes centuries of 'tapasya' or good karma for one to reach that stage where one finds his guru. Blessed are those who are able to find that 'connect' in this lifetime.

441.　When AND is possible, why settle for OR.

442.　Sometimes, we need to go down a few grades to learn something new.

443.　We have two choices: Either focus on what we 'don't have' and keep cribbing all life, or focus on what 'we have' and look at life with abundant gratitude.

444.　Unless you know what you want, you can't ask for it.

445.　When sex is not mere seeking of the body, but a culmination and expression of your deepest love to your beloved, because it enables you to forget yourself in the presence of the other, it gains a spiritual dimension.

446.　Of all the creations, man alone by the way he lives his life, can make this world a little better than it was when he was born.

447.　Though everybody seem to know the 'what to say' part, unless one learns the 'how to say' the 'what to say' part, one cannot succeed in the prevailing world.

448. Between the hater and the hated, it is always the hater who gets hurt more. So forgiveness is not liberating the other from you, but liberating yourself from the other.

449. What happens to you is not in your control, but how you process what happens to you is completely in your control.

450. What failures can teach, success cannot; and what success can teach, failures cannot.

451. Sometimes, you have to step back in order to step forward, and in it you will feel the renewed energy.

452. The bullet that had left the gun cannot return to the gun. It has to hit the target.

453. Do not take care of the body to look good, but to feel good.

454. Spiritual evolution will reveal to you that the highest technique is to have no technique.

455. The feeling that my problem is worse than your problem, so you must give me regard, is in fact a subtle form of ego.

456. Never be like a footballer to kick the ball just for their goal, and kiss the cup. Instead, kiss the one which helped to attain your goal.

457. Let us use our intellect to appreciate the abundance and ignore the negligible scarcity in life.

458. The glory of life is in the chapters to come.

459. Not everything 'can' be measured and not everything 'should' be measured.

460. Don't run after beauty, money and fame. They don't last forever. Go after something that will, like the true love.

461. If I have to ask, 'why me' for all my troubles, then shouldn't I also be asking, 'why me' for all my blessings.

462. The value of 100 rupees is 100 rupees only—not less, not more. But the value of 1 hour depends on who uses that one hour.

463. If intellect is born out of logic, our instinct is born out of Him, who resides within us.

464. Love is, when your intentions are trusted irrespective of your actions.

465. Waking up every day and not having to hear a bad news is itself a great blessing.

466. Happiness is when what you think, what you say and what you do are in harmony.

467. Even if we carry good intentions to correct others, only if we carry respect

in our words, will they look up to us and accept our messages in their life.

468. Always say what you think, but, think before you say it.

469. If you ignore a cub when it is a cub, one day you will have to face the grown-up lion. If you don't face a challenge when it is a challenge, one day you will have to face the grown-up problem. All the problems you face today were the small challenges of yesterday, which you overlooked.

470. Create your own dictionary of words and expression by replacing 'limited vocabulary' with 'resource vocabulary'.

471. The first step to adulthood is to assume complete responsibility for your life.

472. Tomorrow we will understand what and why we went through what we went through today.

473. Nothing will be mine unless I am convinced that it belongs to me.

474. Relationships are like seeds—they have to be nurtured and developed. Expectations are like weeds—they grow on their accord.

475. We all become what we become in life because someone believed in us much before we began to believe in ourselves.

476. We were put on earth for one purpose and that is to make it a better place. And if the earth, as a result of our having been on it, is a better place than it was before we came, then we have achieved our destiny.

477. See your married life like the shape of a diamond. Both husband and wife go in individual directions to find their success, but meet once again to find a common purpose—a happy family.

478. However secure it may be, there is no meaning in remaining a seed in the bottle.

479. Some people meditate in life. For some, life itself is meditation.

480. Every man has the capacity to be an architect of a new world.

481. Forgetting the old is probably as important as remembering the new.

482. An organization not being compatible with your personal needs and necessities does not make the organization wrong.

483. You are 100% responsible for 50% of any relationship.

484. Even a stone, over time, gathers vibrations and becomes a symbol of divinity.

485. Information is nothing more than mental garbage, if it doesn't transform an individual.

486. Sometimes it is not a mere 'yes' or 'no' but the intention and the quality of thoughts behind that 'yes' or 'no', that makes all the difference.

487. It is not punishment that transforms people, but it is love and renewed trust that actually transforms people.

488. If you give your best behind the scenes, life will capture the perfect frame for you.

489. Alive or dead, let the world remark, "There I met an original man, who did not remind me of anybody else, I have ever seen."

490. Without getting things within you right, nothing outside will become right.

491. Getting our thinking right is the sure-fire way of getting our life right.

492. Beauty isn't about how you look, but it is about how you make others feel in your presence.

493. Challenge actually obliges you, for when conquered, they help you to chase greater challenges and in turn provide you greater growth.

494. Inspiration is only the start; It takes dedication, focus and hardworking to see a finished line.

495. Healthy mind and healthy body are the signs of healthy living.

496. A true champion not only wins the award but also the hearts of those who didn't make it.

497. By refusing to accept life's reverse gear, we throw ourselves in top gear.

498. One of the disasters that make humanity decomposes is 'we really don't know what we really want'.

499. A person carrying a heavy load is fine as long as he keeps moving. The minute he stops, the load gets heavier and the distance to be travelled seems greater.

500. Even if your life is not going right, if you continue to grow right, your life will eventually become right.

INDEX

Keyword	Thought no.

A

ability	32,51,203,217,302,322,411
able	9,128,152,214,222,361,411,440
absent	189
abundance	276,324,443,457
accelerate	248
accept	6,110,119,146,170,174,324,359,361, 411,467,497
accord	252,440,474
accountable	139
accumulate	195,325
achieve	68,78,177,180,214,222,314,394,476
action	2,140,257,318,464
activity	92
actor	28
actual	96,107,161,175,331,487,493
adapt	289
add	71,261,334
adequate	184

Keyword	Thought no.
adjacent	14
adjust	289
admire	164
adopt	393
adulthood	471
adventure	149
affect	363
affirm	419
age	116,248
ahead	223,376
aim	12,194,228
align	126,140,293,373
alive	489,161
allow	4,168,186,269,396,422
alone	36,196,414,446
alphabet	235
alter	370
altogether	108
amount	71,184
anger	123
angle	380
angry	347
another	31,67,230
answer	114,267,349

Keyword	Thought no.
anxious	398
apologize	191
appear	2,124,415
appreciate	23,166,210,217,384,457
approach	119
appropriate	322
architect	257,480
area	116
arm	29
art	201
ask	216,228,406,444,461
aspect	425
aspire	68
assign	298
associate	335
assume	471
attach	173,255
attain	456
attention	173,177,296
attitude	13,27,236
attract	32,155,284
automatic	76,144,250
available	220
avoid	42,123

Keyword	Thought no.
awake	73
award	496
aware	285,412
away	136,202,251,258

B

baby	346
back	55,85,120,376,402,438,451
background	260
bad	60,98,329,342,465
badge	70
balance	298
ball	456
bar	431
base	387
basic	173,184
bask	37
battle	323
beauty	77,203,264,322,339,384,419,460,492
bed	256,413
begin	118,186,264,312,397,404,436,475
behave	75
behind	41,195,280,388,432,486,488
belief	126,163,190,215,264,282,315,411, 415,419,424,475

Keyword	Thought no.
belong	53,154,473
beloved	445
benefit	158,393
best	44,50,54,55,61,125,216,300,333,380,413,488
bestow	381
beware	86
beyond	52,95,196,275,390
big	42,75,180,232,323,360,363
billion	28
bird	346
birthday	11
bitterness	247
blame	420
bless	67,270,305,440,461,465
blissful	110
blossom	393
board	258
body	113,118,180,248,284,289,403,429,445,453,495
book	76,101,253,331,353,440
boredom	207
born	81,94,102,187,260,446,463
both	241,255,262,326,414,416,477
bother	276

Keyword	Thought no.
bottle	478
bring	306,318,421
broke	380
brother	285
brush	379
built	304,358
bull	202
bullet	452
burn	232
busy	131,349
buy	43

C

call	177,370,373,408
canvass	379
capable	53,65,84,95,260,303,480
capture	488
card	14
care	453
career	104,281
careful	180
carry	467,499
catch	368
cause	30,66,200,208,225,292,321,339,416, 429

Keyword	Thought no.
celebrate	31,173,209,221
centuries	440
certain	156,187,241
chair	400
challenge	122,179,198,201,237,245,265,268,275,305,345,359,415,469,493
champion	390,496
chance	6,115,230,231
change	62,103,119,143,181,355,389,420
chapter	458
character	129,150,257
chase	493
chatter	437
cherish	210
child	3,82,165,208,231,284,269,285,304,336,345,387,388,413
choice	56,181,250,443
choose	25,32,116,211,373,420
church	285
circle	380
clarify	91
clean	130
climb	63
clock	56
coach	185,214,222

Keyword	Thought no.
coffee	8
coffin	284
comb	43
come	310,350,458
comfortable	62,273
commitment	175
common	477
communicate	91,152,182,288,322,344,394
community	68
compare	194,381
compatible	482
competence	66
competition	431
complete	132,241,266,298,351,449,471
complex	219
concentrate	47
concept	361
concern	225,263,315,393
condition	326,438
confidence	358,412
confuse	248
connect	343
conquer	13,493
conscious	97

Keyword	**Thought no.**
consequence	286
consider	283,301
conspiring	296
constantly	103
contain	349
context	152
continue	10,110,158,401,432,500
contract	224
contribution	158
control	42,231,390,449
convince	202,473
cook	316
cooperate	180
core	150
correct	134,168,467
cost	112,311
count	439,166
country	399
courage	266,286,336,376
course	2
cradle	284
create	53,79,95,98,110,158,195,209,237,242 ,265,307,361,432,435,437,446,470
creature	30,105
cribbing	443

Keyword	Thought no.
criticism	174
crop	64,159
crowd	315
crush	228
cry	347
cub	469
culminate	445
cultivate	64
cup	8,456
cure	200
cute	38
cycle	62

D

daily	371
danger	30
dare	18,169
date	331
daughter	68
daunt	198
day	49,164,183,256,261,285,375,465,469
dead	129,284,489
deadline	335
dear	242

Keyword	**Thought no.**
debate	257
deceive	267
decide	153,232,351,433
decompose	498
decorate	284
dedicate	307,371,494
deep	57,358,445
defeat	16,359,436
define	6,35,271,295,303,417,435
degree	410
delivery	322
demand	345
demonstrate	408
denial	155
depend	35,240,268,290,291,318,363,410,462
deplete	123
depress	436
depth	118,437
design	207,401
desire	54,87,218,378,394
despise	378
despite	379
destination	8
destiny	476

Keyword	Thought no.
destroy	30,98,416
destructive	247
determine	52,128
develop	49,79,359,474
devote	97,140
diamond	477
dictionary	470
die	69,102
difference	4,35,49,54,90,108,171,266,321,392, 486
difficult	45,136,227,332,415
digest	352
dimension	35,445
diminish	37,226
direction	35,266,477
dirt	130,232
disappointment	45
disaster	498
disability	51
discipline	345
discourage	392
discover	122,237,274,280,338
disease	173,296
disobey	150,176,211
disrespect	3,176

Keyword	Thought no.
dissatisfy	107
distance	499
distract	32
disturb	5,291,363,405
divine	343,484
dog	222
door	26
drama	246
dream	58,85,68,167,315
drink	8
dump	228
dustbin	228

E

earning	104,131
earth	30,192,298,340,418,476
easy	232,337,352,433,436
eat	14,180,316,352,366
economy	262
educate	68
effect	321,339
effort	85,262,307,359
ego	219,244,337,405,455
elder	352
elevator	240

Keyword	Thought no.
embody	37
emerge	73,390,418,437
emotion	105,155,173,367,420
empty	209
enable	186,445
encounter	153
encourage	68,392
end	78,80,201,312,336,380,404
enemy	86,106
energy	66,123,149,451
engage	116
engine	369
enhance	32,226
enjoy	8,113,195,233,280
enough	49,221,267,365,366,393,399,425,439
enslave	202
entitle	435
environment	428
envy	30
erase	101,439
error	121
especially	118
essential	185
evens	357

Keyword	Thought no.
event	45,49,80,192,265,404,500
everyday	312
evidence	146
evil	243
evolution	299,454
exactly	346
exam	117
example	50
excellence	4,172
exercise	115,348
exist	98,197,237,282,335,372,378
expand	146
expect	33,75,107,119,148,251,345,474
experience	24,63,78,103,243,283,296,304,328, 355,374,408
expertise	86,154
explain	191,279
expose	154
express	113,218,334,445,470
eye	134,160,249

F

face	29,42,146,188,345,469
fact	122,127,351,357,455
factor	52

Keyword	**Thought no.**
fail	13,89,127,169,249,328,410,430,450
fair	263
faith	39,99,146,186,190,198,336,377,411
fake	267
fall	29,249,277
false	71
fame	460
family	22,68,300,391,477
far	24,79,121,284
fatherhood	429
favorite	237
fear	89,146,155,169,208,249
fed	219
feedback	174
feel	51,57,103,181,189,234,429,436,451,453,455,492
fewer	193
fight	3,208,225,338,418
finally	68,127
find	70,102,113,167,193,201,218,307,334,347,353,391,440,477
fine	256,499
finish	374,494
firm	165
first	27,159,170,235,254,319,362,471

Keyword	Thought no.
flat	29
floor	413
flow	291,409
fly	346
focus	32,97,149,192,292,443,494
follow	315,341
food	184,226,316
foolish	251,325
foot	54
footballer	456
force	163,181,282,390,418
forest	52
forever	60,460
forge	268
forget	131,167,240,349,445,481
forgive	100,448
form	59,67,108,211,321,324,455
fortunate	72
forward	54,451
founder	211
fountain	37
fragrance	384
frame	488
free	272
freedom	25,132,217

Keyword	Thought no.
fresh	348
friend	18,216,300,311,353,380,403
front	265,271,438
fulfill	66,252,341
full	298,390
fun	8
fund	396
future	169,281

G

gain	5,57,218,445
game	336,382,386
gap	107
garbage	73,485
gather	484
gear	497
genuine	323
gesture	182
gift	11,41,46,50,183,203,319,429
girl	68
glass	134,268
glory	458
goal	87,456

Keyword	Thought no.
god	10,34,39,96,126,140,179,186,189, 285,293,328,334,349,364,373,375, 420,434
good	50,60,71,83,98,113,120,130,177,184, 185,232,243,271,287,288,307,308, 329,332,333,342,353,415,436,440, 453,467
grade	442
grateful	186,196
gratitude	443
gravity	140
great	24,46,129,185,217,331,353,359,425, 465,493,499
groom	415
grow	13,49,52,64,71,102,117,164,190,241 ,249,250,299,327,369,469,474,493, 500
guarantee	341
guest	227
gun	452
guru	134,343,422,440

H

habit	410
hair	43
half	28,396
hammer	268

Keyword	Thought no.
hand	10,98,232,254,284,333,353,402
handle	198,415
happen	110,156,180,307,344,419
happy	2,24,74,97,153,182,225,239,283,265,283,294,314,316,334,336,371,407,425,435,466,477
hard	151,315
hardworking	494
harm	415
harmony	466
hate	448
havoc	30
head	229,281,400
headache	200
health	113,115,139,177,184,187,235,311,316,495
heap	73
hear	465
heart	2,41,70,87,182,229,233,289,341,394,401,496
heat	181
heavy	499
heed	395
helicopter	63
help	34,91,117,122,179,196,198,210,313,332,348,431,456,493

Keyword	Thought no.
hence	173
hesitate	18
hide	73,320
high	88,231,354,454
history	21,246,365,390
hit	10,414,452
hold	202,267,284,405
holy	253,440
home	29,35,269,297,424,427
honest	286
honor	70,175
horizon	197
hour	228,285,462
house	427
huge	73,155
human	13,69,77,94,98,173,224,246,381,390, 419,498
hundred	425
hurt	416,448
husband	3,477

I

idea	252,308
identify	66,261
ignore	96,243,351,457,469

Keyword	Thought no.
image	434
immediate	188
impact	284
imperfect	148,199
implies	127
important	157,253,292,335,356,388,481
improper	288
improve	149,217,312,382
inability	324,430
incompetence	84
increase	115
indeed	274
individual	485,477
inferiority	219
infinite	169,303,320,381
information	485
ingredient	427
inhale	140
initially	267
inner	334,437
insecure	25
inside	10,320
insights	57
insignificant	265

Keyword	Thought no.
inspiration	181,323,494
instinct	155,346,463
instrument	167,383,409
intellect	457,463
intensity	60
intention	108,251,372,464,486
interest	116,232,429
invention	280
invest	157,162,295,384
involve	298,379
ironically	21
irrespective	56,286,330,464
irritate	436
issue	3
item	14

J

jeopardize	400
journey	111,149
joy	371
judgment	217,260

K

karma	440
kick	456

Keyword	Thought no.
kid	29,50,424
kind	31,33,165
kiss	456
know	57,96,157,222,300,309,323,346,373, 412,424,426,444,447,498

L

lack	191
land	73
language	178
large	66,410
last	60,341,362,460
late	46,417
later	113,305
laugh	193
law	213,378
lay	87,353
lead	45,69,121,163,255,269,275,281,282, 333,359
learn	86,104,159,186,308,346,360,442,447
least	253,395
leave	95,110,192,195,272,388,432
left	135,452
legacy	95,432
less	23,72,366,382,415,462

Keyword	Thought no.
lesson	186,328,360
level	415
liberate	448
license	3
lie	129,214,322
life	6,7,15,51,58,65,72,75,81,83,88,92,94, 100,101,102,103,110,111,117,121, 122,124,132,141,142,143,156,158, 173,180,181,186,187,196,203,207, 210,220,221,226,231,232,241,251, 261,265,272,284,300,308,330,332, 336,343,348,351,353,356,357,360, 364,381,386,389,401,404,408,409, 415,421,425,443,446,457,458,467, 471,475,477,479,488,491,497,500
lifestyle	177
lifetime	95,156,195,208,368,399,440
lift	21
light	181,436
like	10,76,101,129,142,246,265,305,327, 345,366,380,421,456,460,474,477
limitation	275,324
line	374,494
linger	251,362
lion	469
lip	182
list	17,375
listen	44,178,344,403

Keyword	Thought no.
little	151,202,208,446
live	30,59,69,81,83,94,95,102,121,132, 158,183,187,230,238,261,264,269, 285,290,309,315,351,352,366, 368,401,432,446,495
load	499
logic	2,105,463
long	49,267,289,323,366,375,409,499
look	90,97,132,135,160,167,199,204,265, 287,348,443,453,467,492
loophole	396
lord	183
lose	19,311,382
loss	417
lost	37
lot	19
love	9,37,72,182,199,238,270,291,367, 370,380,417,422,427,445,464,487
loyal	400

M

magic	177,413
maintain	130,298
maker	21
man	22,31,65,95,105,131,141,144,202, 204,218,220,237,243,313,329,347, 365,369,434,446,480,489

Keyword	Thought no.
manage	27,317
mankind	383
manners	287
marathon	374
marriage	74,118,125,131,307,337,477
master	5,322,368
masterpiece	361
material	41
mathematician	380
matter	2,22,126,179,250,253,264,413
mature	45,123,250,393
me	31,100,183,244,342,419,455,461,473,489
mean	24,100,108,112,176,189,211,276,285,376,344,407,478
measure	380,459
meditate	479
meet	477
member	297
memory	233,265,413
mental	115,485
menu	14
mere	247,284,445,486
mess	130
message	238,467

Keyword	Thought no.
met	31,489
midnight	232
million	30,329
mind	48,70,87,108,188,219,248,267,289, 355,436,495
minute	499
miracle	267
mirror	160
misappropriate	396
misery	110
miss	11,46,47,81,230,317,329,368
mistake	168,277,340
modify	177
moment	8,76,156,209,210,337,423
money	98,460
monotony	207
mood	56,420
mother	38,346,406,429
motivate	56
mount	63
mountain	13
move	109,258,385,430,499
multiply	306
music	409

Keyword	**Thought no.**
my	100,139,183,194,285,295,364,370, 380,393,436,455,461,473

N

name	373
nation	68
nature	173,155,419
necessary	178,298,332,342,482
need	55,60,78,140,157,159,165,180,186, 197,210,218,229,241,252,266,293, 342,371,389,395,403,422,442,482
negative	247,439
negligible	457
nest	346
new	98,159,186,197,211,428,442,480,481
news	465
nice	271
noble	372
noise	437
notice	23,256
nuclear	383
nurture	474

O

oblige	493
observe	185

Keyword	Thought no.
obvious	54
offer	364
office	23
oil	232
old	116,145,159,211,215,428,481
open	26,91
opportunity	230,254,317,320,402
opposite	345
optometrist	134
oration	322
order	14,186,241,451
ordinary	4
organization	369,400,482
original	31,489
ornate	284
ought	351
ourselves	4,34,181,245,282,423,475,497
outlook	389
outside	10,204,490
overburden	245
overcome	208,220
overflow	182
overshadow	155
own	65,72,128,242,249,252,297,315,327,398,401,421,431,435,470

Keyword	Thought no.
oxygen	140

P

Keyword	Thought no.
pace	109,430
pack	322
pain	335,374
paint	361,379
pair	134
paper	54,117
paradigm	215
paralyses	155
parent	82,165,257,336,345,387
parenthesis	320
part	300,447
partner	148
pass	198
past	247,327,339,374,421,437
pause	322
pawn	258
peace	78,100,219,294,301,325,371,405
peak	248
people	15,46,155,160,164,206,210,223,225,239,270,275,279,280,315,329,363,367,393,395,415,479,487
perceive	275

Keyword	Thought no.
perception	59,401
perfect	148,199,298,347,488
performer	55
period	357
permission	4
person	14,47,70,104,108,118,178,205,234, 293,294,308,332,410,435,499
personal	232,363,410,482
personality	79,259,435
philosophy	281
physical	115,158,432
pick	29
piece	258
pill	177
place	29,49,233,264,269,297,424,476
planet	340
plant	49,159
play	16,28,35,246,336,382
please	293
pleasure	116,335,374
point	26,194,245,305,365,417
policy	356
poor	22
pose	267
positive	129,188,231,439

Keyword	Thought no.
possess	72,218,383
possible	155,169,280,394,441
pot	10
potential	52,175,303,329,381
power	65,175,258,383
practical	206
practice	206,211
pray	15,23,60,183,256,364,375
precedence	104
precise	366
prefer	384
presence	103,445,492
present	189,254,349
preserve	325
prevail	447
prevent	169
price	191,232,311
priority	104
private	423
probably	481
problem	17,47,97,136,219,220,299,367,381, 455,469
proceed	328
process	87,139,172,449
produce	439

Keyword	Thought no.
product	201
professional	79
progress	78,295,301,328
promote	255
proper	115
property	423
prophet	368
protect	352,367
proud	310,399
prove	408,411
provide	203,241,359,493
public	423
pull	159,193
punctuate	322
punishment	415,487
purchase	325
pure	387,422
purpose	261,334,394,476,477
push	346
put	54,206,248

Q

qualification	281
quality	50,58,77,103,185,191,318,379,436, 486

Keyword	Thought no.
quantum	92
queen	258
question	33,61,114,165,263,267,312,349,362, 393

R

rabbit	109,430
raise	431
rare	31
ration	203
reach	8,117,284,313,440
react	420
read	108,21,133,185,336
real	33,146,271,498
realize	147,167,202,311,420
reason	193,366,425
reborn	81
receive	53,132,227
receptive	48,393
recipe	352
recognize	41,205,330,334
reconnect	212
recruit	79
reflection	82
refused	73,497

Keyword	**Thought no.**
regard	455
regret	121
reject	164
relate	118
relation	30,47,118,132,234,288,291,326,343, 358,393,438,474,483
relaxed	248,355
relevant	114
religion	211,212
remain	73,354,409,478
remark	31,489
remember	38,101,224,481
remind	31,489
renew	401,451,487
repeat	207,408
repent	147,417
repetitive	207
replace	63,391,470
repulse	255
request	375
require	17,66
reside	463
resist	110
resolve	136,399
resource	220,252,317

Keyword	Thought no.
respect	217,387,467
respond	51,290,302
responsible	51,65,114,139,141,142,302,379,414, 420,471,483
rest	21,184,224,330,372
restart	186
restless	248
result	172,476
retrieve	262
return	452
reveal	275,454
reverse	497
revolutionary	150
rhythmically	409
rich	22
right	7,33,92,117,134,144,162,184,197, 204,263,308,333,351,353,429,433, 490,491,500
rise	277
risk	19
road	414
rob	219
role	28,35,246
root	49,159,212
rope	202
rose	384

Keyword	Thought no.
rough	198
routine	371
row	438
run	136,202,266,374,460
rupee	228,462

S

sacrifice	232
sad	407
safer	264
salt	131
say	13,18,44,76,255,308,366,380,447,466,468
scarcity	192,196,457
scariest	30
scene	488
scratch	124
script	162
search	239,255
seat	438
second	50
secret	18
secure	25,90,278,478
see	14,41,160,181,186,197,204,215,220,268,329,411,477,489,494

Keyword	**Thought no.**
seed	49,52,73,102,276,418,474,478
seek	66,349,445
seem	155,305,327,368,421,447,499
self	71,149,247,304
selfishness	218
sell	43
send	120
sense	132,194
sentence	108
serve	122,288,316,334
set	280
settle	25,441
sever	288
several	280
severe	415
sex	445
shape	10,477
share	72,218,273
shatter	268
shift	236,292
shortcut	213
show	238
side	148,380
signal	359
sign	495

Keyword	Thought no.
silence	273
simple	54,182,352,360,390
sincere	23,60,85
sing	256
sister	285
sit	285
situation	42,153,188,220,281,381,420
skill	27,382
slave	25,202
sleep	303,413
slow	369,385
small	75,97,265,360,363,434,469
snail	109,430
social	224
sofa	413
soft	229
soil	49,102,418
solution	17,281,350,367,395
solve	17
some	15,423,479
someday	417
sometime	55
son	406
song	129

Keyword	Thought no.
soul	285,331
source	323
space	125,296,297,371
speak	7,178
special	156,233
specialization	154
spectacle	124,197
speech	304
speed	56,369
spend	368
spirit	40,69,152,285,290,432,445,454
spite	249,376,379
spontaneity	437
sprout	276,418
stage	28,55,421,440
stair	240
stand	249,397
standard	117,431
start	97,119,131,137,166,196,281,361,494
starve	219
state	78,248
station	8
stay	32,49,272,278,376
steel	268

Keyword	Thought no.
step	169,170,223,451,471
stifle	122
stock	220
stone	484
stop	57,166,221,359,420,437,499
storm	198
story	101,336,396
strength	40,272,350,428
stress	188,302
strong	229,274,359
struggle	79,219
student	83,117,161
study	208
stuff	237
subconscious	296
subject	57,83
sublime	343
subtle	455
succeed	54,208,447
success	20,54,85,109,125,127,209,221,223, 242,328,334,341,387,410,450,477
suffer	186,219
sugar	131
suggest	365
sun	37

Keyword	Thought no.
sunrise	1,46
sunset	1
superior	219
support	210,300,424
support	10
surprise	251
surrender	244,412
survive	292
sustain	118
symbol	484
system	168,293,396

T

table	14
tag	311
take	19
talk	145,367
tantrum	151
target	280,452
task	298
taste	352
teach	36,83,114,161,450
tears	350
technique	454
tell	100,206,234

Keyword	**Thought no.**
temple	285
tense	248
tenth	117
term	381
test	117,415
thank	186,328,375
thing	97,129,154,200,262,270,308,311,330, 338,345,360,490
think	14,38,129,130,188,207,210,275,350, 355,361,375,436,466,468,491
thorn	384
though	447
thought	139,231,383,486
threat	292
throw	151,228,299,497
tick	56
tide	354
time	7,26,27,50,60,92,97,104,130,151,156, 157,177,190,191,194,206,220,223, 251,253,262,289,293,295,305,308, 311,328,351,357,362,367,371,384, 402,421,484
today	55,59,106,171,210,245,264,280,295, 310,312,469,472
together	21,252
told	210

Keyword	Thought no.
tomb	133
tomorrow	106,171,245,295,310,398,472
tool	175
top	63,369,497
total	424
touch	394
tough	386,433
towards	119,170,389
train	188,222,369
trait	150,324
transform	170,485,487
transition	62
travel	8,499
treat	313,403
tree	49,73
trial	121
triumph	326
trouble	80,131,268,292,461
true	125,202,257,327,411,426,460,496
trust	146,279,411,464,487
truth	215,255,420
try	89,96,149,152,277,359,361,402
turn	127,402,365,493
twice	13

Keyword	Thought no.
two	181,443

U

ultimate	194
unburden	48
uncertainty	241
unconditional	370
uncountable	30
understand	36,88,96,152,270,300,344,358,393, 472
unearth	49
uneasy	436
unfair	415
unhappiness	225,306,314
unhappy	407
uninvited	227
unique	31,246,435
universe	163
unjust	415
unknown	169,320,373,437
unlearn	159
unlimited	246
unproductive	123
unselfish	218,393
untouched	437

Keyword	Thought no.
unwritten	224
use	240,270,334,402,457,462

V

value	100,128,147,178,334,356,462
vertical	154
viable	351
vibration	484
victorious	304
view	71,124
vision	134
vital	427
vocabulary	470

W

wake	46,413,417,465
want	34,415
warmly	227
waste	130
way	36,90,108,120,164,183,219,238,269,329,348,393,415,420,433,434,439,446,491
weak	40,190,272,274,350,428,436
wealth	115,235,283
weapon	383
wear	259

Keyword	Thought no.
weed	64,276,474
welcome	29
well	323,344,352,355,390
whisper	18
whole	246,369,400
wife	3,477
willpower	359
win	16,382,496
window	76
wise	226
wisher	323
womb	278
won	89,228,323,386,390,419
wonderful	77,162
word	76,182,212,235,322,344,467,470
work	23,39,256,334,364,373
workout	184
workplace	391
world	11,21,28,31,98,77,98,119,144,149, 154,158,195,204,239,264,315,319, 324,334,347,361,365,392,397,420, 446,447,480,489
worry	99,384,398
worse	455
worth	34,76,194,205,252,338

Keyword	**Thought no.**
write	101,108,290
wrong	7,127,129,184,216,234,307,433,482

Y

yesterday	59,171,264,469
yield	2
young	145